ideas for DECOUPAGE and DECORATION

Dedicated to our parents.

ideas for DECOUPAGE and DECORATION

Betty Lorrimar and Margaret Hickson

 VAN NOSTRAND REINHOLD COMPANY
NEW YORK CINCINNATI TORONTO LONDON MELBOURNE

Van Nostrand Reinhold Company Regional Offices:
New York Cincinnati Chicago Millbrae Dallas

Van Nostrand Reinhold Company International
Offices:
London Toronto Melbourne

Library of Congress Catalog Card Number: 74–6793
ISBN: 0–442–30070–0

This book is set in Monophoto Bembo and
printed in Great Britain by Jolly & Barber Ltd, Rugby.

Published by Van Nostrand Reinhold Company,
450 West 33rd Street, New York N.Y. 10001 and
Van Nostrand Reinhold Company Ltd.,
Molly Millar's Lane, Wokingham, Berkshire

16 15 14 13 12 11 10 9 8 7 6 5 4 3 2 1

**Library of Congress Cataloging in Publication
Data**

Lorrimar, Betty.
 Ideas for decoupage and decoration.

 Bibliography: p.
 Includes index.
 SUMMARY: Describes the tools and techniques of
decoupage with instructions for projects.
 1. Decoupage – Juvenile literature. 2. Design,
Decorative – Juvenile literature. 3. Decoration and
ornament – Juvenile literature. [1. Decoupage.
2. Handicraft] I. Hickson, Margaret, joint author.
II. Title.
TT870.L73   745.54   74–6793
ISBN 0–442–30070–0

Contents

Acknowledgements

The authors would like to thank students whose work is shown. We are also grateful to those who allowed us to photograph them while carrying out the practical activities involved. We acknowledge help and permission to reproduce items from the following collections: Mr. Kenneth Hickson; *The Sunday Times;* The Victoria and Albert Museum, London; Museum für Natur- und Völkerkunde, Basle, Switzerland.

An attractive string print on paper, see page 40.

Fig. I–1. Two spectacular examples of decorative work from
New Ireland, in the Pacific. Patterns and animal forms were used
to create these works which were almost always carved from a
single plank of wood. Reproduced by permission of the Museum
of Ethnology (Museum für Natur- und Völkerkunde), Basle.

Fig. I-2. An example of a decorative Polish folk-art paper cut-out
from the late nineteenth century; several pasted together make an
attractive frieze.

Introduction

In an age of mass production, in which the free play of creativity is all too often replaced by the pre-fabricated and the pre-sold, an increasing number of people every year are turning away from the anonymity of manufactured designs and artifacts. They are seeking to give their surroundings a personal touch by embellishing them with original, rather than store-bought, decoration.

However, a mass of technical problems confronts the beginner who wants to decorate his own furniture. What kinds of surfaces are best suited for decoration? Where can they be obtained? How should they be prepared? Which are the simplest methods of decoration, and what materials do they require? What are the technical errors to be avoided?

The purpose of this book is to answer questions such as these, so that you can try your hand at decoration with a full measure of confidence. Of the many decorative techniques, we have chosen eight: decoupage, leaf printing, string printing, collage printing, monoprinting, stencilling, sgraffito, and painting. These have been selected because, while simple enough for the beginner, they offer a wide scope to the artistic imagination.

We have not exhausted the possibilities of any of these methods, but have chosen rather to outline the best and most reliable procedures for someone just starting out. After you have mastered the techniques in this book, you will probably want to learn others or, better yet, come up with ideas of your own.

Most of the methods discussed are ideal for children, and in fact many of the illustrations have been selected from work executed in schools. Throughout we have emphasized, not the kind of work which is found in museums (and which the beginner could hardly hope to emulate), but rather the sort of results which anyone can obtain with a little practice.

We hope this book will be of use to anyone starting out in the exciting field of creative home decoration.

Betty Lorrimar
Margaret Hickson

Fig. I–3. A Norwegian armchair in pine, carved and painted red, blue, green and yellow. Made by C. G. Christensen and exhibited at the Paris Exhibition in 1900. Reproduced by permission of the Victoria and Albert Museum, London.

1. Finding and preparing objects

Finding objects to decorate

Before we discuss the 'how' of decoration, the 'what' must be considered. You may not have an object on hand which is suitable for decoration, or you may wish to start by experimenting on an expendable item. So the first problem to be dealt with will be where to obtain such items.

Junk shops are among the best and cheapest sources for objects to decorate. Even pieces which at first sight appear somewhat delapidated can often be transformed by cleaning and a bit of repair. For example, the rocking chair in fig. 1–1 was very shabby when originally purchased; but after the blemishes were treated and the surface repainted, it became an attractive piece of furniture. However, when buying from junk shops you should be careful to avoid wood that is either rotten or infested with insects.

Jumble sales and markets can also be useful places for finding objects. Always bear in mind that even an unattractive piece can be put to good decorative use.

Cheap whitewood (that is, unfinished) furniture is readily available in shops and, even though mass produced, can be given an individual appearance through careful decoration.

Relatives and friends are often eager to dispose of unwanted items, which can then be restored, cleaned, and decorated. Similarly, you may be able to obtain pieces of discarded school equipment, such as broken desks and chairs, tins and boxes used for delivering supplies, and so on.

Finally, a search in your own attic, garage, or garden shed may uncover suitable objects. Sometimes a slight alteration can provide a new function for something

Fig. 1–1. Decorated rocking chair.

that has lain unused. For example, the legs of a table can be shortened to convert it into a coffee table, or an old chest can be used as a desk or dressing table. There are many such possibilities.

Suitable paints

Having chosen your object, the next step is to prepare it for decoration. However, before putting on the background colour you should give some thought to the type of decoration you intend to use.

A flat or eggshell finish is a good ground for decoupage and for all types of painted or printed methods. The work can then be carried out in enamels, lacquers, tube oil colours, printing inks (oil, emulsion, or water based), gouache, acrylic paints, or glued paper.

If an enamel is to be used for the surface finish, avoid tube oils or gouache, as it will be difficult to apply them to a shiny base. The oils are liable to flake off or to dry improperly. Acrylics, lacquers, and other enamels can be used in their place.

Tempera and oil paints are often painted over a gesso ground. Gesso is whitening or plaster mixed with glue, and can be readily obtained from artists' suppliers. It is applied after the wood has been cleaned. About three coats are brushed over the object, and each coat must dry thoroughly before the next is applied. All types of paint can be used on a gesso ground. It is a sound, long lasting base, as is indicated by the durability of old paintings whose creators worked on gesso.

Preparing whitewood

Unfinished pieces of furniture can be bought at reasonable prices from most large stores (fig. 1–2). They are ideal for any kind of decoration. To prepare whitewood for decoration you will require the following materials:
Old newspapers.
Fine sandpaper.
Primer paint or shellac.

Fig. 1–2. Whitewood chest.

Undercoat (that is, flat paint of the same colour as the final coat).

Brushes.

Thinner and brush cleaner (turpentine).

(Note: The following instructions should be read in conjunction with the sections on the care of paints and brushes, pp. 55–61.)

If you are working indoors, you should cover the floor with newspapers. Begin by sanding the wood carefully with fine sandpaper; this ensures a smooth finish by removing the rough spots which are often found on cheaply produced items. In the process you will also get rid of any grease marks or dirt.

After sanding, wipe the surface of the wood with a damp cloth (fig. 1–3). Be sure to remove all traces of dust before applying the undercoat. (It is advisable at this point to remove the newspapers in order to dispose of sawdust, and lay down fresh papers before beginning to paint.) The surface is now ready to receive its first coat. Sandpapering will have created a good gripping surface, so that the paint will adhere properly without blistering or cracking.

14   *Fig. 1–3. Rubbing down after sanding.*

Fig. 1–4. Applying the primer.

Before going any further, apply a coat of primer paint. This serves to seal the pores of the wood. It gives a flat finish (that is, without shine) and helps to fill in the thirsty grain of the wood. A coat of shellac may be used if preferred. It is important to allow primers adequate time to dry and harden before applying further coats of paint.

Before brushing on the undercoat, sandpaper the surface again lightly. This second coat should also have a flat finish, so that it will be easy to apply the final coats. Use light, even strokes, brushing horizontally from left to right, and then from right to left (fig. 1–4). Be careful not to overload the brush with paint.

The final coat before you begin to decorate should also be a flat or eggshell finish, as it is easier to put on a design if the surface is not too shiny. Before applying the last coat, another light sandpapering will enable the paint to grip well and evenly. Remember to allow each coat of paint to dry thoroughly before applying the next one. The maker's instructions as stated on the container should be carefully observed.

Preparing older wooden objects

Wood that is old, or that has been previously stained or painted, should be prepared with great care for decoration. In addition to the materials required for preparing whitewood, you may need these items:

Waterproof abrasive paper.

A scraper or blunt knife.

A commercial paint stripper.

All dirt, grease, and wax must be removed from the surface. To do this, wash the wood down with soap and water or detergent solution. Rub the surface while it is still wet with medium grade waterproof abrasive paper. The surface should then be rinsed well and left to dry.

Some objects will have been painted many times over with thick paint. A scraper or blunt kitchen knife can be used to remove defective or poorly adhering spots. If you wish to remove the old coat entirely, the work can be speeded by using a commercial paint and varnish stripper, obtainable at any hardware or paint supply

Fig. 1–5. *Removing paint with a commercial stripper.*

Fig. 1–6. *Scraping off stubborn layers of paint.*

Fig. 1–7. Sanding to remove grease and rough areas.

store. Most such products contain harsh, caustic, sub-
stances, and great care must be taken when using them.
It is a good idea to wear rubber gloves (fig. 1–5). These
products should not under any circumstances be used
by children. The work of the commercial stripper can
be supplemented by the use of a scraper (fig. 1–6).

When the old finish has been removed, wash the object with soapy water and leave it to dry. It should then
be sandpapered to provide a good gripping surface for
the paint (fig. 1–7). When dealing with very rough
wood, a coarse glass paper can be used first, followed by
a fine grain sheet. Do not forget to wipe down after-
wards.

The primer can now be applied, in order to seal the
wood and enable the subsequent coats to dry evenly
(fig. 1–8). When the primer is dry, you can attend to
any cracks, nail holes, scratches, or other blemishes

Fig. 1–8. Applying the primer.

17

that mar the surface. These can be filled in either with plastic wood or with special types of filler obtainable from hardware stores. Apply the filler generously, as these products shrink somewhat when they dry (fig. 1–9). After the filler has hardened, sand the surface again (fig. 1–10) and wipe down to remove dust (fig. 1–11).

Now you can apply an undercoat of the appropriate colour. The number of coats required before putting on the final finish depends largely on the type of decoration to be used; in some cases, only one may be needed.

Preparing metal

Metal is an equally suitable surface for decoration. You will need the following materials to prepare it:

    Rust remover.
    White spirit or garlic juice.
    Fine grain sandpaper.
    Metal primer.

Before you decorate a metal surface it must be free from rust. Commercial rust removers can be obtained at garages or car accessory shops. After removing the

18   *Fig. 1–9. Filling in defects with a commercial plaster filler.*

Fig. 1–10. Sanding after the filler has hardened.

Fig. 1–11. Wiping down before applying the undercoat.

rust, you can eliminate grease by rubbing the metal with white spirit and a little whitening powder. Garlic juice (which was used by Renaissance painters) or methylated spirits are suitable for the same purpose. Finally, the surface should be washed with soap and water, rinsed, and dried as quickly as possible. If the metal has been previously painted, sand it well before washing.

After cleaning thoroughly, sand the surface with fine grain glasspaper. The object should now receive a coat of metal primer or clear varnish.

There are several methods of decoration you can use once the varnish has been applied. If you wish, you can work directly on clear varnish with crayons made for that purpose (available from artists' suppliers). If, on the other hand, you want to work on a coloured ground, brush on two or three coats of flat paint. Allow at least a day for drying after each coat, and sand the surface gently before you apply the next coat.

The metal is now ready for decoration. Japan based colours work best with metal (see colour plates 3 and 4, pages 26–27). Japan is a drying agent which, when added to oil paint, helps it to dry quickly and so prevents dust from forming on the surface. You can buy paints ready mixed with Japan from most hardware and paint stores. The resulting finish will be hard and glossy, so that varnishing will not be necessary.

Acrylic paint can also be used, but you may find it more difficult to apply smoothly. Small tins of lacquer are another possibility; the ease with which they can be manipulated makes them particularly suitable for children.

2. Methods of decoration

Decoupage

Decoupage is the art of decorating surfaces permanently with paper cut-outs. (The name is derived from the French word 'couper' – to cut.) The technique evolved in eighteenth-century Italy, and soon spread throughout Europe, reaching a height of popularity in the nineteenth century. In recent years there has been renewed interest in this method, which permits a wide range of decorative effects.

Originally, decoupage was used to imitate the appearance of hand-painted Chinese and Japanese lacquer work. 'Japanned' furniture had become so popular that importers were unable to meet the demand. Designers began to substitute paper cut-outs for the original hand painting, as a result of which decoupage was sometimes referred to as 'poor man's lacquer'. Leading artists and designers, such as Boucher, Wattea, and Pillement, provided engravings for use in decoupage. Books containing prints specifically designed for decoupage were published on a wide scale. These were cut out and pasted to objects, which were then lacquered. The layers of varnish disguised the fact that the prints were pasted on, so that many antique examples of decoupage appear to have been painted by hand. Birds, flowers, and insects were among the favourite motifs of early decoupage artists.

Decoupage is sometimes confused with two other related methods of assemblage: collage and montage. Collage, like decoupage, makes use of paper cut-outs, but in addition it has recourse to other materials, such as string, cloth, wood, etc. Montage, on the other hand, involves the juxtaposition of different photographs, sometimes with the incorporation of brushwork, to create a new image. The finished product can then be rephotographed to create the illusion of a single photograph.

Fig. 2–1. Cabinet decorated with pictures from quality magazines. 21

You will need the following materials for decoupage:
Scissors (curved cuticle scissors are best for cutting
out rounded and detailed shapes).
Cellulose or clear drying paste or glue.
Varnish or lacquer.
A soft cloth.

One of the most appealing aspects of decoupage is the
limitless range of imagery you can choose from. Any
number of separate cut-outs, in any combination, can
be used for your decoration, so that the usual problem
is not to find suitable material, but to choose from
among the vast number of possibilities.

Here are a few suggestions for where you might start
looking; but you will find as you go along that when it
comes to finding fresh motifs for decoupage, the only
limit is your imagination. If you want to emulate the
effect of antique decoupage, you can find old illustrations in print shops and museum bookstalls. Similar
material can be found in magazines dealing with art or
history (figs. 2–1 and 2–2). Seed catalogues are a useful
source of floral motifs (see colour plates 1 and 2, page
26), while wallpaper sample books offer a variety of
colours and textures (see colour plate 5, page 27).

Popular magazines have the advantage of being in-
expensive and easily obtainable. By looking through a
number of magazines you will be able to accumulate
material on whatever theme you have chosen (fig. 2–3).
For example, pictures of food can be used to decorate
kitchen furniture (see colour plate 6, page 27), or a chest
for a young boy's room can be embellished with illustrations from sports magazines (see colour plate 11, page
35). If you want to repeat a motif, you can buy several
copies of the same magazine. If you are relying on
advertisements, you will find that the same ones often
appear in several different magazines.

In general you will get the best results with thin paper.
However, when there is printing on both sides, as in a

Fig. 2–2. Bedside cabinet decorated with historical motifs.

*Fig. 2–3. Umbrella stand decorated with pictures cut from
magazine covers.*

magazine, there is a danger of the other side showing through when the picture is pasted down. You can test for this by lightly dampening the back with water.

If you do intend to use thicker paper, it will be necessary to mix the paste into a pulp-like consistency and apply it generously.

You may need a little practice at first to get the feel of cutting. As we have noted above, small cuticle scissors are best for decoupage; they enable you to handle intricate details and curved edges. Go slowly at first, holding the paper firmly in one hand and manipulating the scissors with the other. If there are interior sections to be cut away, do these first. Once you have mastered the technique of cutting, you will find that it can be a very relaxing pastime.

In order to be able to work without interruption, you should have all the pictures you will need on hand and already cut out before you begin the job of pasting (fig. 2–4).

As far as choosing an object is concerned, you should start out with something small. A large table or cabinet might take months to finish, and would hardly be a suitable starting point for someone just learning the techniques of decoupage.

If the work is to be carried out on a wooden or metal object, the surface should be prepared as described in the first pages of this book. It is very important to seal the pores of a wooden surface; otherwise the grain will soak up the paste and the decoupage will fall off.

If you prefer, you can begin by covering the whole area of the object with a cut or torn paper background (figs. 2–5 and 2–6). Paste the background on with the same glue you will use for the cut-outs. When all or part of the surface is covered with pieces of paper cut to size, paste the cut-outs on over them. Otherwise, if you intend to apply the cut-outs directly to the surface of the object, put a coat of flat or eggshell finish paint over the undercoat and primer. Stainers should not be used, as the cut-outs will not adhere well to these.

For fastening the paper to the surface you should use

Fig. 2–5. Whitewood chest covered with brown paper, prior to applying a decoupage design.

Fig. 2–4. Floral cut-outs for use in a decoupage design.

25

Colour plate 2. Chest with decoupage flower decoration ; see page 23.

Colour plate 1. Chair with decoupage flower decoration ; see page 23.

Colour plate 3. Metal jug and plate, painted with Japan based colours ; see page 20.

Colour plate 4. Metal pot and bowl, painted with Japan based colours; see page 20.

Colour plate 5. Tray decorated with simulated wood paper; see papers; see page 23.

Colour plate 6. Kitchen chest decorated with decoupage, using magazine pictures of fruit; see page 23.

27

Fig. 2–6. Preparing a base pattern.

Fig. 2–7. Applying coloured papers to a prepared surface.

cellulose or a clear drying paste or glue. Apply the glue quite liberally to the back of the paper, spreading it evenly over the whole area so that the paper will have a smooth surface when glued down.

Having glued the back, press the paper down carefully, working from the centre of the shape out to the edges so as to avoid air bubbles and creases (fig. 2–7). A soft dry cloth can be used for this. Do not rub the paper; this can smear the printing on the cut-out. Gentle pressure will usually eliminate air bubbles. If necessary, you can carefully lift off the paper before the glue dries and reapply it.

A certain amount of excess glue will probably ooze out at the edges when you are pasting down. This can

Fig. 2–8. The first layer drying before further pieces are applied.

be removed with a cloth moistened with warm water. Vinegar can be substituted if the glue has begun to dry.

When superimposing different pieces of paper, each layer should be allowed to dry before applying the next (fig. 2–8). When pasting is completed and the last layer has dried, brush over the surface with a clear varnish or lacquer. How many coats you apply will depend on the effect you want. Early decoupage artists used as many as ten or fifteen coats, sanding lightly between each layer, so that eventually no cut edges could be seen or felt. However, one or two layers of good quality varnish will be enough to protect the surface. The varnish will enable you to polish the object when necessary without damaging the decoupage.

Fig. 2–9. Tray decorated with simulated wood papers; note the use of geometric shapes to form patterns.

Items decorated with decoupage are quite durable, making this a suitable method for embellishing almost any object in the home: chests, wall panels, doors, trays, boxes, etc.

There are several other ways in which paper can be used to decorate furniture. Gummed papers (available from artists' suppliers) can be applied directly to a surface (see colour plate 16, page 39). By choosing papers of different colours and cutting them into geometric shapes you can create a wide variety of patterns (fig. 2–9). Gummed papers can also provide a base on which cut-outs can be superimposed. Varnish will protect the decoration.

Interesting effects can be obtained by using coloured tissue papers (see colour plates 8 and 9, page 34). Since the papers are transparent, colour mixing will result when papers of two different colours are overlapped. Varnish, in addition to protecting the surface, will help to prevent the colours from fading.

Monochrome (that is, the use of different shades of a

Fig. 2–10. Decorated screen with newsprint background. Group work by children aged 13.

31

Fig. 2–11. Chest decorated with leaf prints.

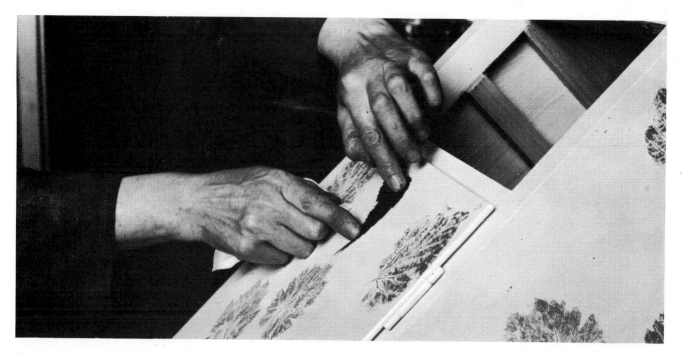

Fig. 2–12. Positioning the leaf.

single colour) also has attractive possibilities. By searching through newspapers and magazines you can compile tonal variations of the same colour, which can then be arranged in abstract patterns.

As you experiment in the area of decoration with paper, you will discover that any number of common materials can be incorporated into your designs to create a collage effect: newsprint (fig. 2–10), gift wrapping paper, postage stamps, bottle labels, etc. These can be combined with any of the above techniques to add variety to your work.

Printed decoration

Of the many methods of printing, we have here chosen several of the simplest. The basic materials you will need for the techniques described below are as follows:

A roller, of a size appropriate to the method you are using.

Printing ink (oil, water, or acrylic based).

An inking slab (any smooth, hard surface).

(1) LEAF PRINTING

Leaf printing can produce very attractive decoration and yet is so simple that even young children can manage it without difficulty (fig. 2–11). Its only limitation is seasonal; the leaves used should be fresh and pliant. Dry leaves will crumble under pressure. You will get

Colour plate 7.
'Noah's Ark':
a painted chest for toys;
see page 55.

Colour plate 8. Tray decorated with coloured tissue papers; see page 33.

Colour plate 9. Landscape made from coloured tissue papers; see page 33.

Colour plate 10. A table decorated by monoprinting with plastic sheets; see page 45.

Colour plate 11. Small chest for a boy's room; it is decorated with decoupage, using plain coloured papers and sports motifs cut from popular magazines; see page 23.

Colour plate 12. A painted screen; see page 55.

Fig. 2–13. Rolling the leaf.

the best results with leaves whose markings are clearly defined. Generally the back of a leaf produces the clearest image.

There are two ways of transferring a leaf print on to a prepared surface. You can lay the leaf, underside uppermost, on a piece of newspaper, and brush over it with the printing ink. Then, lifting the leaf carefully, press the painted side carefully into position on the surface to be printed (fig. 2–12). The pressure applied should be gentle, so as not to blur the image. You can do this by hand, or you can use a soft cloth, a paper towel,

or torn newsprint. When you peel off the leaf you should have a clear print. However, if you have not brushed on enough colour, your print will be uneven. Similarly, if too much colour has been applied, the print will be murky and the veins of the leaf will not show.

An alternative method of printing leaves is to use a roller for applying the colour to the leaf (fig. 2–13). Spread the ink on a piece of thick glass or other smooth surface, and use the roller to transfer the colour to the leaf. Then continue the printing process as described

Fig. 2–14. Leaf print executed on paper.

above. It is best to print one colour at a time, allowing each to dry before putting on the next; otherwise, smudges will result.

When you first try your hand at leaf printing, it is a good idea to practise on paper in order to discover the right pressure for producing a clear, even print (fig. 2–14). By experimenting with a variety of leaves you will find which ones produce the best results for the effect you are seeking.

Many types of colour can be used. If you are working on paper, water based paints or printing inks are suit-

able. These can also be used on furniture or walls, as they can be varnished when the print is completed. Tube oil colours or printing inks give good results, but take longer to dry. Another possibility is emulsion printing medium, which, while washing easily off rollers, brushes, and hands, becomes waterproof after about two days.

If you are using leaf printing to decorate furniture, you may be interested in printing curtains and cushions to match. The leaves can be applied to fabric in the same way as to any other surface, using either oil based

Colour plate 13. Printed plastic roller-blinds; see page 75.

Colour plate 14, left. Painted chest for a child's room; it is painted with scenes from 'The Three Bears'; see page 55.

Colour plate 15, right. Chest decorated with string and collage prints; see page 41.

Colour plate 16. Tray decorated with coloured gummed paper; see page 30.

Colour plate 17. Painted pianos by students of the Royal College of Art. Copyright: The Sunday Times; see page 75.

Colour plate 18. A decorated guitar; see page 75.

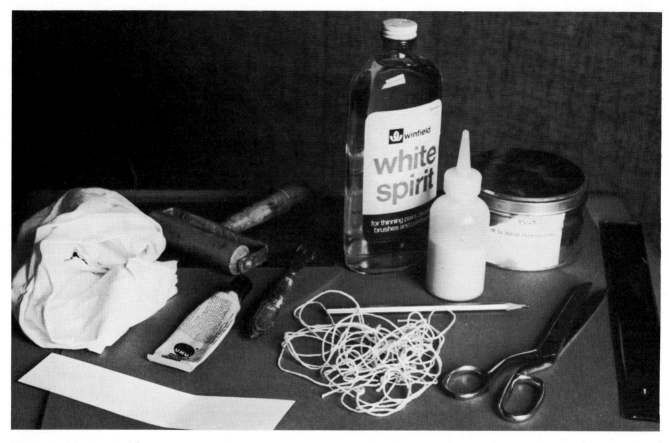

Fig. 2–15. Items required for string printing.

colours or tubes of fabric dye (obtainable in artists' supply stores).

Leaves are not the only organic materials suitable for printing. Grasses and ferns print very clearly, and some vegetables (such as potatoes, carrots, and onions) can be used to create interesting textures. Before colour is applied to any of these, moisture should be blotted so that the ink is not rejected.

(2) STRING PRINTING

String printing is a slightly more elaborate technique, appropriate mainly for smaller areas such as wood panels. In addition to roller and ink, you will need white resin glue, a ball of string, and thick paper or thin card (fig. 2–15). The latter should be sufficiently pliable to enable you to control it while printing.

Begin by cutting a piece of thick paper or thin card to the size of the surface you are decorating. Having planned your design, draw it on the paper with strong

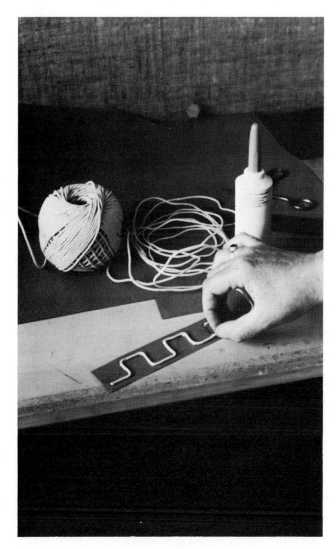

Fig. 2–16. Arranging string on the glue base.

white resin glue. (A container with a nozzle will make it easier to execute small details.) Then place string over the glued outlines and press it down firmly (fig. 2–16). Soft string is preferable for this. For best results the string should not be too taut. You should also make sure that the string is the same height at all points in order to print evenly. (When choosing string you should consider its texture, as this will register in the print.)

After the string is in place, allow the glue to dry thoroughly so that the string will be fixed firmly in position. Next, use the roller to cover the string design with ink, and press the paper down firmly on the surface to be decorated so that the string lines will register. Be careful to avoid sliding the paper while you are pressing it down.

The use of string will restrict you to relatively simple linear patterns. As noted above, the nature of this technique is such that it is not really suitable for very large areas. You should of course bear in mind when laying out your design that in the finished product it will be reversed, as in a mirror.

(3) COLLAGE PRINTING

A collage print is made by gluing a variety of different materials side by side on a piece of card, so that when printed a multitextured design results. Any materials are appropriate, from wool to wallpaper (fig. 2–17), so long as their textures will register. However, they must all be of the same depth in order for the ink to print evenly. The printing procedure is the same as for string. If you wish, you can use the roller to press the paper on the surface you are decorating (fig. 2–18).

If the print does not come out properly, it can be removed instantly with a turpentine saturated rag (if oil based colour has been used) or with a damp sponge (if you have used a water based medium).

Techniques can be combined to great effect; for example, string and collage prints work well together as you can see in colour plate 15, page 38.

(4) MONOPRINTING

The earliest monoprints date from the seventeenth

41

Fig. 2–17. Collage using wallpaper, by a child aged 12.

Fig. 2–18. Pressing down the block using a roller.

century. The Italian painter Giovanni Castiglione is said to have originated the concept of making a unique print by drawing in ink or paint on one surface and pressing the design (while still wet) on to another surface. Despite the favour this technique found with such artists as William Blake and Edgar Degas, monoprinting has never been widely practised, chiefly because only a single print can be made and the results are to an extent unpredictable.

However, monoprinting is an ideal technique for those with a taste for free and spontaneous styles of design. Unlike decoupage or the other types of printing we have discussed, it does not require a great deal of advance planning. Enamel, oil, or acrylic paints are the best mediums for this form. As for the surface on which the original drawing is executed, any number of materials have been employed in the past, such as glass, wood, or metal. However, for printing on furniture it is best to use a more pliable material. We have found plastic sheeting to be most suitable (fig. 2–19).

Cut the plastic to the size and shape of the area to be decorated, and lay it down on a hard surface. (Keep an ample supply of newspapers around; monoprinting can be a messy process.) Paint your design on the plastic (fig. 2–20). You can use a brush for this, or else dribble and splatter the paint from

Fig. 2–19. Sheets of plastic for monoprinting.

44   *Fig. 2–20. Painting on the plastic.*

Fig. 2–21. Laying the painted plastic on the surface to be decorated.

the can, depending on the effect you want to create.

In monoprinting, unlike most printing methods, you can use any number of colours simultaneously. The main problem to watch out for is applying the paint too thickly, since the paint will spread out when the plastic is pressed down for printing. Unwanted paint can be removed from the plastic with a rag soaked in turpentine. When you have finished painting, lift up the plastic gently, while the paint is still fresh, and lay it down carefully on the surface you are decorating (fig. 2–21). Rub the back of the sheet (not too roughly) to

transfer the design to the surface. Then, very delicately, lift the plastic at one end and peel it off (fig. 2–22). When dry the completed monoprint can then be varnished for protection (fig. 2–23) to give you an idea of the colours used in this project see colour plate 10, page 35.

In another variation of this method, you can use a roller to apply a coat of paint to a sheet of plastic, and then scratch out a design with a pointed object. Then, if the paint has not been applied too thickly, you can make a print of this scratched design by the same process described above.

Fig. 2–22. Peeling off the plastic.

Stencilling

In one form or another, stencilling has been practised since virtually the dawn of art. It was used in Ancient Egypt and in the China of the Chou Dynasty; it was familiar to the Fiji Islanders and to the Tlingit Indians of Alaska. It has been employed to embellish everything from temple walls to kitchen utensils. In effect, stencilling was one of the first forms of printing; in medieval Japan it was used to reproduce religious texts. The earliest known European playing cards (in the fifteenth century) were printed with stencils, as were the first manufactured wallpapers of the seventeenth century.

Stencilling remains an excellent method of printing, particularly if you wish to repeat the same motif a number of times, either in a picture (fig. 2–24) or on a piece of furniture (fig. 2–25). There are knives, brushes, and paper specifically designed for stencilling which are sold in art supply stores. However, non-absorbent paper or thin card may be substituted for stencil paper, and any firm brush can be used to apply the colour.

Work out your design in advance on drawing paper. The style should be bold and simple, since the pattern will have to be cut. Excessively fine details will make the stencil too fragile for carrying out the printing.

When the pattern is complete, trace or draw it on the

Fig. 2–23. Coffee table top decorated with monoprinting.

47

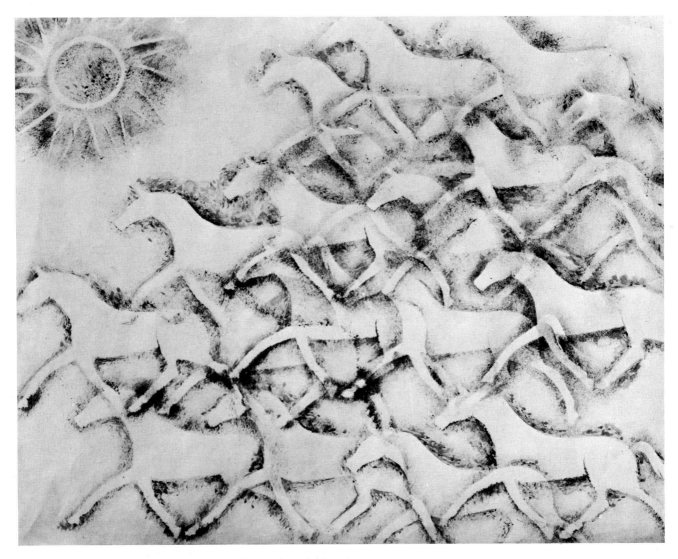

Fig. 2–24. A repeat of galloping horses; a stencil picture by a child aged 14.

Fig. 2–25. Stool with stencilled base pattern.

Fig. 2–26. Cutting the stencil.

Fig. 2–27. Trying out positions for stencilled motifs.

stencil paper. Then place the paper on a hard surface, such as metal or thick glass, and cut away the parts to be printed, using a sharp stencil knife (fig. 2–26). Some designs can be cut with scissors. A separate stencil is needed for each colour you intend to use.

Any type of paint can be used. Place a small amount of each colour in a saucer or other similar container. The paint should be neither too thick nor too fluid. It is best to print the lightest colours first.

You can use the portions that have been cut out to position the pattern on the object to be decorated (fig. 2–27). When you are ready to paint, fix the stencil in position with masking tape. If the design is small enough it can be held down with one hand. Then stamp or brush the paint through the open parts of the design

with a stencil or ordinary brush (fig. 2–28). The brush should be as dry as possible. You can make an ink pad for the same purpose by wrapping a piece of cloth around a sponge or ball of wadding, and tying it at the top.

Lift the stencil off slowly and carefully, so as not to smudge the edges of the design (fig. 2–29). This procedure should be practised on paper before you try it on objects.

You can also stencil using the reverse of the method described above; that is, by taking the section cut out of the stencil paper and painting around it. These two methods can be combined in the same decoration.

As with the other techniques we have described, the stencilled decoration should be varnished after it is dry.

Fig. 2–28. Using the stencil brush.

Fig. 2–29. Lifting off the stencil.

Sgraffito

Sgraffito (from the Italian for 'scraped') is a word used to describe any technique in which portions of the finish are scraped away in order to reveal the surface underneath. The technique reached its height in the Renaissance, when many church frescoes were created with sgraffito. In that era the top coat was generally white plaster, which was spread over a tempera undercoat. However, the same principle can be applied by a variety of means.

The simplest method is to paint a surface and then, with a sharp knife or gouge, cut or scrape the paint while it is still wet in order to form a pattern. The original surface (on the scraperboard) will then be exposed in the scraped areas (see fig. 2–31 for an example of a scraperboard).

Alternatively, you can give the object a preliminary coat and, when it has dried, apply a second coat of a different (preferably darker) colour. This second coat is then scraped to reveal the colour underneath. In any case, the relief should not be so pronounced that dirt or dust will accumulate in the indentations.

Another form of sgraffito is to cover the surface with wax of one or more colours. The whole is then covered with black wax, which can be scraped away with a sharp tool to reveal the wax beneath (fig. 2–30).

By a related method, burning can be substituted for scraping. Draw the pattern carefully with a heated tool such as a soldering iron. The scorch marks which will show at the line edges can be quite attractive. (If you prefer, the burning can be done directly on untreated wood.) However, this technique requires careful execution, and is not suitable for children unless they are supervised. It should be carried out slowly and in a well ventilated room.

Fig. 2–30. Wax sgraffito design.

Fig. 2–31. A scraperboard, by a child aged 13.

Painted decoration

Painting directly on an object is the most fundamental technique of decoration and can give some wonderful and varied results (see figs. 2–32, 2–33, 2–34, 2–35, 2–36, 2–37, 2–38, and colour plates 7, page 34, 12, page 35, and 14, page 38). It would be far beyond the scope of this book to talk about the craft of painting in all its aspects; that is obviously an area about which many thousands of books have been written, and if you have decided to try your hand as a painter you will have already given some consideration to the aesthetic side of it.

However, in this chapter we will leave inspiration and artistry to one side and offer a few mundane, but very important, tips about painting. It is all too easy to overlook details such as the proper care of a brush or the temperature of the room in which you are painting, but they can radically affect the ultimate appearance of your work. Painting is in some ways the most simple and direct method we will discuss in this book, but it is essential to pay careful attention to the technical points outlined in the following pages.

(1) TRANSFERRING DESIGNS TO THE PREPARED SURFACE

When you are planning a painted decoration, you will probably want to work out your design on paper beforehand. The design can then easily be transferred to the surface to be decorated. After you have drawn your pattern to scale, trace it on to detail or tracing paper, preferably using a soft (2B) pencil. Then cover the back of the tracing paper with either white chalk (if the background on which you will be working is dark) or with charcoal (if the background is light). Fix the tracing in position on the object. (Masking tape is best for this, as it will peel off without removing paint when the paper is taken away.) Taking a harder pencil (HB), draw over the lines of the pattern. The chalk or charcoal will transfer the design to the surface.

If you are working on a large area, tracing small areas at a time will prevent the lines from smudging or smearing. When the pattern has been transferred, the chalk or charcoal lines can be painted over with a light water colour paint to make them more durable. The water colour can then be washed off after the guide lines have served their purpose.

(2) CARE OF PAINTS

You can store paint for a considerable time as long as a few simple directives are followed:

(a) Paints should not be kept in very hot or cold places, as they will be adversely affected by extremes in temperature. Make sure that the lids or caps are firmly sealed so that air cannot enter.

(b) Before using the paint again, check to see if it has acquired a skin. If it has, remove the layer of skin. If this is done carefully, the skin should come off in one piece. As a further precaution, the paint can be strained.

(c) Stir the paint thoroughly if this is recommended by the manufacturer.

(d) When thinning, be careful not to do so to excess. Use the proportions of thinner to paint indicated by the manufacturer, and only employ the type of thinner which is suited to the particular paint being used.

(e) Oil paints that are left over can be allowed to remain on the palette, as long as they are submerged in water between painting sessions to prevent the paint from hardening. To clean the palette after you have finished painting, wash it with linseed oil.

(f) Tube acrylic paint can also be kept ready for use by submersion in water between painting sessions. With this type of pigment it is very important to seal the can or tube firmly. The paint quickly hardens if it is not kept airtight.

(3) CARE OF BRUSHES

Good quality brushes, if properly cared for, will give years of service. However, if you do not clean your brushes after use they will be ruined by hardening of the bristles. It takes only a few minutes to remove the paint and clean the brush so that it will remain in good condition. Here are a few points to remember:

(a) When using a new brush, it is wise to dip it into

Figs. 2–32 and 2–33.
Two painted stools, showing the
possibilities of using free
brush strokes for decoration.

clean turpentine before you start. Having done this, make a few backward and forward strokes on a clean board or similar surface. This will remove loose bristles, which are found in even the most expensive brushes.

(b) The paint container must be the correct size for the brush. Forcing a six-inch brush into a three-inch can will bend the bristles out of shape and ruin the brush.

(c) If you take a work break, don't leave the brush in the paint can; this will cause the bristles to bunch together. If your brush has a hole at the top of the handle, as many do, you can run a rod or wire through it and leave the brush suspended in a jar or tin when not in use. When using oil paints, it is a good idea to put turpentine in the jar to prevent the brush from drying out. Before painting again, make a few backward and forward strokes on a clean surface to remove the excess turpentine.

(d) After using oil paints, wash the bristles with turpentine; then wash them again in warm water, and rinse thoroughly. Soap will remove any paint still caught in the brush. After shaking the water out, taper the tips of the brush with your fingers to help the brush retain its shape.

(e) When using emulsion or acrylic paint, soap and warm water are sufficient for cleaning the brush.

(f) Brushes should dry in a suspended position. If there is no hole in the handle, you can loop a string round it to suspend the brush.

(g) If you are not going to use the brush again for some time, rubbing a little lard or petroleum jelly into the bristles will help keep them supple.

(4) PAINT TROUBLES

Most of the flaws which may arise in a painted surface can be traced to easily avoidable mistakes. We have listed here some of the commonest problems. A reasonable amount of care will usually prevent them from occurring.

Bittiness

If you paint with a dirty brush, the bits of extraneous matter will adhere to the surface. The same thing can happen if skin is not carefully removed from the paint before use. To remove fragments of skin, you can if necessary strain the paint.

If you find you have accidentally applied a bitty finish, allow it to harden and then sand it down. If its appearance is still not satisfactory, put another coat over it.

Blistering

Paint will blister (that is, fail to adhere to the surface in spots) if it is applied to damp or unseasoned wood. Extremes of temperature change, or a hot sun continually beating down on the surface, will intensify the blistering.

This defect may also occur if a second coat is applied before the first has dried sufficiently. A third cause of blistering is the formation of moisture between the layers of paint. This can be avoided if you do not paint in a damp atmosphere or in direct, hot sunlight.

Blooming

The shine of varnish or gloss paint is sometimes spoiled by a misty or hazy effect – known as blooming. This can be caused by bad ventilation, damp air during the drying process, or air pollution. Rubbing the surface with strong vinegar and polishing with chamois leather will counteract blooming to some extent. Scrubbing and washing will also help to restore the shine.

Slow drying

There are many causes of poor drying. Excessive humidity, dampness, and stagnant air all work against the drying process. If the surface being painted has not been cleaned thoroughly, so that wax polish or bituminous material remain, the paint will not dry satisfactorily. Insufficient light delays the drying of paints containing oil.

Fig. 2–34. Delicately painted English screen made in 1746. Reproduced by permission of the Victoria and Albert Museum, London.

59

Paint dries best when applied in a warm, dry atmosphere. If, as a result of bad conditions, it does not dry after a prolonged period, the only solution is to remove the defective coat and apply another. Before repainting, check to make sure that the problem was not caused by greasiness.

Crazing

Crazing (irregular cracking or splitting of a painted surface) may be due to the application of hard drying paint or varnish over soft or oily undercoats. Painting before the undercoat has dried will also produce this effect.

Sometimes a crazed appearance is deliberately sought, in order to imitate the cracks of antique decorated objects. You can achieve this quality simply by working over a damp undercoat.

Sinking

If a coat is applied to a porous surface, or to one that has been insufficiently primed, it will dry mat (without shine) because the paint will sink in. The application of further coats will remove this defect.

Wrinkling

Using paint too thickly will cause a surface skin to form on the thicker spots, thus preventing them from drying evenly. Always remember to paint smoothly and not too generously.

Poor opacity

If paint is applied unevenly, or if the paint has been thinned excessively, the undercoat or undersurface will show through the finishing coat. The same will occur if the undercoat is darker than the finish. If you want to paint over a darker undercoat, it may be necessary to apply many coats.

Flaking

Paint will peel if dirt and grease have not been fully removed from the surface before painting. It is important to make sure that all surfaces are clean and dry before covering them.

None of these defects need occur, so long as you observe the above points and follow the manufacturer's instructions carefully.

Antique effects

Painted or varnished decorations can be given an antique appearance by a comparatively simple method. The result is often quite attractive, especially if your design has an old-fashioned quality.

The antique effect is achieved by substituting, for the two coats of clear varnish that would normally be applied to protect the decoration, a special finish which will alter its appearance. This finish is a mixture of clear varnish, a tiny amount of linseed oil, turpentine, and raw Turkey umber. The proportions of the ingredients should vary according to how dark a glaze you want. The standard mixture would consist of three parts Turkey umber and turpentine to one part clear varnish, with one drop of linseed oil added. To darken the glaze, add more umber. Raw sienna oil colour can be substituted for umber if you want the finish to have a warmer quality.

The painted decoration must be completely dry before the finish is applied. The work of applying it must be carried out very quickly. After the mixture is brushed on, it must be immediately rubbed off with a soft cloth. It is safer to treat one small area at a time. More linseed

Fig. 2–35. 'Bathers in a Landscape' by Vanessa Bell, executed 1913–1914; a modern painted screen. Reproduced by permission of the Victoria and Albert Museum, London.

62   *Fig. 2–36. A small chest painted with moonlight scenes.*

Fig. 2–37. A 'picture-book' painting of 'The Three Bears' story, on a small chest; see colour plate 14, page 38.

64

oil can be added to prevent the glaze from drying too quickly, but this is not usually necessary.

If the glaze does not turn out properly, wipe it off with turpentine before it is completely dry.

When the process has been completed, let the surface dry, and then cover it with a coat of clear varnish for further protection.

This type of finish can have a softening effect on the colours of a design, so that colours which would normally clash blend together more harmoniously. To enhance the antique effect, this technique can be combined with the method described in the preceding chapter, by which cracking can be induced through painting over a damp undercoat.

Care of decorated objects

Varnishing an object after completion (whether the decoration is decoupage, printed, or painted) creates a surface which is quite durable. When necessary, it can be cleaned with damp chamois leather. A normal wax or silicone polish will also help to preserve the surface and prevent marking or scratching.

After several years, the shine of the finish may fade, giving the surface a dull appearance. Warm water mixed with either soap or a mild detergent may then be used to clean it. If this fails to remove all grease, sponge the surface with methylated spirits. You can then restore the shine and freshness of the colours by applying a fresh coat of clear varnish. When you have finished, the decoration will have nearly regained its original appearance.

Fig. 2–38. An antique painted cabinet designed by William Burges, made in 1858. Reproduced by permission of the Victoria and Albert Museum, London.

3. Design

Designing is really the choosing and arranging of shapes, lines, and spaces in between. Ideas for making patterns are all around us. You can sit in a room and contemplate the environment; you may notice wood grain markings on doors and furniture, reflections, shadows, and numerous other textures and shapes. Personal interest and inclination will determine which of these will interest you. Outside even more examples can be seen: tree branches silhouetted against the sky, rough bark on tree trunks, roof tiles, and buildings.

Looking for sources can be very interesting. Pick out those you find most attractive and make simple drawings of them. This may appear difficult at first but after a little practice you will soon get the idea. A felt tipped pen or marker will give the best results as you will be unable to put in unnecessary details.

Here are three pairs of illustrations (figs. 3–1 to 3–6); in each case the first sketch suggested a decorative design for a piece of furniture. Try other sources yourself and make similar sketches for your own designs. Remember, you are designing instinctively every day when you arrange your furniture, lay the table, and choose what you will wear for the day.

When you have created an attractive result it can be drawn on to your object. You may then paint it or do the design in decoupage, using coloured papers or tapes.

66   *Fig. 3–1. Pile of logs.*

Fig. 3–2. Sketch for a chest with a design inspired by logs.

Fig. 3–3. Pen and ink drawing of tree roots by a child aged 15.

Designing in this way can lead to a renewed interest in your surroundings and encourage you to train your eyes to observe more closely.

Colour

Many people, when they begin to experiment with decoration, find the problems of mixing and combining colours very forbidding. It is true that, if you begin by working with a large palette and splashing on colours in haphazard combinations, the results are not likely to be attractive. However, you can discover how to obtain the effects you want by starting modestly, working with only a few colours at a time, and bearing in mind the rudiments of colour mixing which we will sketch in this chapter. To simplify, we will talk in terms of painting, but much of what follows is equally relevant to decoupage or any other form of decoration.

As far as pigments are concerned, there are three primary colours: yellow, red, and blue. These three can be combined to form all the other colours of the spectrum. For example, orange is obtained by mixing yellow and red; violet, by mixing red and blue; and green, by mixing yellow and blue.

The direct derivatives of the primaries (orange, violet, and green) are known as secondary colours. These can in turn be used for mixing to produce yet more colours, so that the range of possible colours is virtually limitless.

In addition, any tone can be lightened by adding white, or darkened by adding black.

You will probably not want to obtain all your colours by mixing, since an enormous variety of pre-mixed colours can be obtained from artists' suppliers. But it is useful to have an understanding of the principles involved in mixing, since these have a direct bearing on the effects of different colour combinations.

The six primary and secondary colours can be divided into three pairs of complementary colours. Two colours are complementary if between them they contain the three primary colours; so that red is complemented by green, yellow by violet, and blue by orange.

In each of these pairs you will find one 'warm' colour (red, yellow, orange) and one 'cool' colour (green violet, blue).

The warm and cool colours have been so called chiefly because of their psychological effects. The warm colours tend to induce a volatile mood, while the cool colours are more calm and immobile.

When warm and cool colours are combined in one composition, a number of optical effects become ap-

Fig. 3–4. Sketch for a cupboard with a design based on tree roots.

Fig. 3–5. Woven basket.

Fig. 3–6. Sketch for a chest with design based on the shapes of woven canes.

69

Fig. 3–7. Geometric patterns on furniture, designed to make up an
attractive grouping.

parent. Warm colours seem to approach the eye, and cool colours to recede from it. You can therefore create a relief effect by setting a warm colour against a cool background. Similarly, objects painted in a warm colour appear to expand, while those painted in a cool colour appear to contract.

Your choice of colours will depend largely on the mood you want to create. You should of course consider not only the combinations within the decoration, but also the way in which the decoration will relate to the other colours in the room.

The essential question in combining colours is finally one of personal taste. Having absorbed the elementary facts of colour, the best way to proceed is to follow your instincts and experiment with different combinations until you find which ones best express what you want to get across.

Repeat patterns

Sometimes a straightforward repeating pattern can produce an effective form of decoration. A number of possible frameworks can be studied, and the chosen one ruled on to the surface on which it is to be painted. Repeating designs can also be printed. Several patterns may combine to form the whole, and they can be divided by plain or patterned borders. Groups can work together to produce a decoration in this way (see fig. 3–7). Before beginning, they must decide on which colours to use; everyone must then use the same colours, so that a unified result is achieved.

The scale of the object must be considered. A very large piece does not really look right with a small pattern on it, and vice versa. It is difficult to state any absolute rules in art and design, however, as they change

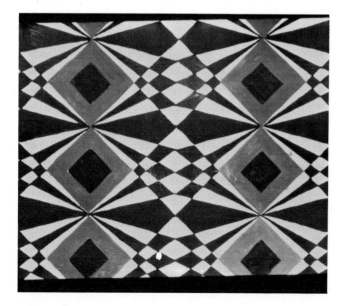

Fig. 3–8. Geometric pattern by a child aged 16.

Fig. 3–9. Pattern formed from several cut-out geometric shapes, by a child aged 15.

with fashion and artists are continually disproving them. The best guide is to say: 'If it looks right, it *is* right' – and leave it at that.

Templates are very useful for repeat patterns. Any shape may be cut out in thin card and then used for drawing round. Geometric shapes (such as figs. 3–8 and 3–9) are easily made by using mathematical instruments. Other shapes can be traced on to the card and then cut out. There are plenty of books and magazines available today from which shapes may be taken and combined to form pleasing patterns.

Lettering

Lettering is in itself decorative (see fig. 3–10). It is often incorporated into design schemes and may be patterned or plain. The beautiful shapes formed by Roman letters cannot be excelled, and most alphabets are based on these.

Lettering is all around us, on shop fascias, signs, packaging, books and posters. It can be seen at its most attractive when it forms part of the decoration on inn signs, roundabouts, fairground stalls, and barges.

Other ideas for decoration

MUSICAL INSTRUMENTS

Decoration on musical instruments is a tradition that goes back a very long way. Many primitive instruments are actually made in the shapes of animals, serpents, or fish, and have appropriate carved or painted patterns on them.

72   *Fig. 3–10. Part of a large decoration using lettering. Group work by children aged 11.*

Fig. 3–11. A decorated piano made in 1865. Reproduced by permission of the Victoria and Albert Museum, London.

73

Fig. 3–12. One way to decorate your guitar; see colour plate 18, page 39.

Sixteenth- and seventeenth-century clavichords were frequently decorated. Some of the paintings on the lids of these instruments were exquisite. One of the most famous works of the seventeenth-century Dutch painter Vermeer shows a woman seated at the virginals.

The nineteenth century produced painted pianos (see fig. 3–11), guitars, drums, organ pipes, and many other decorative instruments in Europe and America. Examples are found in all parts of the world, Siamese bands being particularly impressive.

Decorating your musical instrument can produce some really marvellous results, as with the guitar (fig. 3–12 and colour plate 18, page 39) and pianos in colour plate 17, page 39.

SHELLS AND DRIFTWOOD

Shells, driftwood, and pebbles have always been used by folk artists, especially those living near the sea shore. They may be used to decorate many objects in the home (see fig. 3–13), or used as inspiration for painting patterns.

PLASTIC

We buy many items that are wrapped in plastic or polythene sheeting. This material has many decorative possibilities. Monoprints are made on plastic, and then printed on to a surface. Large sheets of plastic can be decorated and used as shower curtains, or for kitchen and bathroom windows (see colour plate 13, page 38). The material lets through sufficient light, and wears well. Attractive wall hangings or space dividers can be made in the same way. Holes may be cut to form interesting patterns, and the plastic can be painted or printed.

Fig. 3–13. Shell collage suitable for a bathroom.

Glossary

Acrylic paint: Generally a water based paint combining pigment and plastic resin, along with other chemical additives to give the paint the proper consistency.

Acrylic paints are used with water, and can be either opaque or transparent; when dry they become waterproof.

Bittiness: The presence of small particles of extraneous matter in a coat of paint.

Blistering: The failure of a coat of paint to adhere to a surface.

Blooming: A misty or hazy appearance which spoils the shine of varnish or gloss paint.

Collage: A technique involving the use of a variety of materials (paper, cloth, etc.) in a single composition.

Crazing: Splitting or cracking of a painted surface.

Decoupage: A technique in which a surface is permanently decorated with paper cut-outs.

Eggshell finish: A sheen on paint, midway between mat and high gloss.

Emulsion: A paint whose vehicle is composed of solid or viscous liquid resin particles in water. When dry it becomes insoluble.

Enamel: A paint based on varnish or on mixtures of varnish and oil, rather than on oil alone.

Filler: A substance (such as plastic wood) used for filling fine cracks or indentations.

Flaking: The lifting or peeling of paint from a surface, usually caused by moisture under the paint.

Flat: A surface without gloss or sheen (also referred to as 'matt').

French curve: An instrument (usually made of wood or plastic) with a variety of curved edges, used for guiding the hand in drawing.

Gesso: A compound used for priming a surface. It produces a brilliant white ground with a high degree of absorbency. Gesso was originally made with gypsum (from which it derives its name), but today the term is applied to a number of different mixtures which produce a similar result.

Gloss: The degree to which a painted surface reflects light.

Gouache: An opaque water colour (also known as 'poster colour').

Japan: A drying agent added to oil paint to assist its drying properties.

Lacquer: A paint that dries rapidly by solvent evaporation.

Matt: See Flat.

Monochrome: Using the tones of only one colour.

Monoprint: A print made by painting with oil paint or printing ink on a shiny surface (such as plastic) which is then pressed on the surface to be decorated.

Montage: A decorative method in which photographs are mounted on a photographic background to produce an unusual, often incongruous composition.

Motif: The repeated element in a pattern.

Paint stripper: A liquid containing strong solvents, used for removing old layers of paint.

Pigment: A colouring substance (of organic or artificial origin) in powdered form. It must be combined with a binding agent (such as linseed oil) to produce a soluble paint.

Primer: A preliminary coat of finish applied to a surface before painting. Its function is to enable the paint to adhere securely to the surface.

Roller: A cylinder used for applying paint to large areas or for conveying ink to the block in printing.

Sanding: The use of an abrasive to level a surface prior to painting.

Sgraffito: A technique in which a design is cut, scraped, or burned into a surface.

Shellac: A resin used in combination with alcohol to provide a protective finish.

Sinking: Uneven absorption of paint, caused when paint is applied to a porous or poorly prepared surface.

Skin: The hard crust which forms on paint and ink when they are left in an open container.

Solvent: The volatile constituent of a paint, which evaporates as the paint dries.

Stencil: A thin plate or card with a pattern cut through it.

Stripping: Removal of old paint or paper.

Tempera: A paint made from a mixture of pigment and an emulsion binder. A combination of egg and water is often used as the emulsifying agent. Tempera paints are usually applied on a gesso ground.

Template: A pattern (usually of wood or metal) which serves as a guide for repeating the same shape.

Thinner: An oily liquid which can give oil paint a more fluid consistency.

Undercoat: The coat of paint applied after the primer and before the finish.

Varnish: A transparent coating composition compounded of drying oils and natural or synthetic resins.

White spirit: A mixture of petroleum hydrocarbons used as a solvent for paints and varnishes.

Wrinkling: The uneven drying of a coat of paint, caused when paint is applied too heavily.

Bibliography

Faber Birren. *Principles of Color: A Review of Past Tradition and Modern Theories.* Van Nostrand Reinhold, New York and London, 1969.

Dorothy Harrower. *Decoupage: A Limitless World in Decoration.* M. Barrows & Co., 1958.

Owen Jones. *Grammar of Ornament.* Van Nostrand Reinhold, New York and London, 1972 (first published 1856).

Norman Laliberté and Alex Mogelon. *The Art of the Stencil.* Van Nostrand Reinhold, New York and London, 1971.

Norman Laliberté and Alex Mogelon. *The Art of Monoprint.* Van Nostrand Reinhold, New York and London, 1974.

Ralph Mayer. *The Artist's Handbook of Materials and Techniques. Revised Edition.* Faber & Faber, London, 1973.

Frederic Taubes. *The Painter's Dictionary of Materials and Methods.* David & Charles, 1973.

Frances S. Wing. *The Complete Book of Decoupage.* Pitman, 1968.

Suppliers

All the materials and equipment suggested for use are easily obtained, and most of them can be bought in large department stores. Specialist shops will of course supply and advise on materials. Below is a list showing the type of store which deals with particular items.

Artists' colourmen and suppliers

Artists' acrylic, oil, tempera, and water colour paints
Fine sable paint brushes
Gesso
Linseed oil
Printing inks
Raw Turkey umber
Tracing paper
Wax and other crayons

Decorating supply or hardware stores

Glues and pastes
Japan based colours
Fillers and plastic wood
Lacquers
Paints – enamels, emulsion, primer, polyurethane etc.
Paint stripper
Sandpaper and scrapers
Turpentine and other paint thinners
Undercoat
Varnish

Index